LENCI DOLLS

IN FULL COLOR

Toys for the Rich and Famous,
1920–1940

by

Helen Nolan

Dover Publications, Inc.
New York

Cover Illustrations

FRONT COVER. Very choice 27″ Lenci Madame de Pompadour, ca. 1927. INSIDE FRONT COVER. Four photographs illustrating the section "The Children" on pages 4–7: (top left) 15″ early Lenci child, with handwritten number (42) on mid-1920s style tag; (top right) 17″ girl with unusually pouty face, mid-1920s (may have been intended to represent Greta Garbo); (bottom left) 14″ Lenci mold 111, mint and unplayed-with condition, 1920s; (bottom right) 17″ pouty girl, probably one of the 300 series, mid-1920s. INSIDE BACK COVER. 21″ doll given to present owner in 1920, intended to represent Mary Pickford. BACK COVER. Same doll as the preceding.

Acknowledgments

With very special and particular thanks to Alice O'Neill Avery and to Lenon H. Hoyte, who kindly allowed some of their dolls to be photographed for this book. With gratitude to Dorothy Coleman for her suggestions and advice (and for the basic research she has already provided the world in the field of Lenci). With appreciation to Signore Beppe Garella of today's Lenci, S.R.I., of Italy, for all his thoughts and his help. And with affection to my sister Pat, who did "business as usual" so I could do books.

About the Photographer-Author

Helen Nolan was an advertising copywriter and creative director in New York City for eighteen years. Ten years ago she also opened an antique doll shop, The Magnificent Doll, Inc., in New York. In 1981, she retired from advertising and moved to Massachusetts, where she now sells antique dolls by mail all over the world.

Published in Canada by General Publishing Company, Ltd., 30 Lesmill Road, Don Mills, Toronto, Ontario.
Published in the United Kingdom by Constable and Company, Ltd., 10 Orange Street, London WC2H 7EG.

Lenci Dolls in Full Color: Toys for the Rich and Famous, 1920–1940 is a new work, first published by Dover Publications, Inc., in 1986.

Manufactured in the United States of America
Dover Publications, Inc., 31 East 2nd Street, Mineola, N.Y. 11501

Library of Congress Cataloging-in-Publication Data

Nolan, Helen.
Lenci dolls in full color.

1. Lenci di E. Scavini (Firm)—Catalogs. 2. Dolls—Italy—History—20th century—Collectors and collecting—Catalogs. I. Title.
NK4894.I8N64 1986 688.7′221′094512 86-23995
ISBN 0-486-25204-3

Introduction

All dollmakers are influenced by their time, and the makers of the fabulous Lenci dolls, created in Italy during the 1920s and '30s, were no exception. What is exceptional about Lenci is the height of artistry they managed to achieve—artistry that was unparalleled by any other manufacturer of the time. What is also unique is that many of these dolls were designed as decorative objects, not as playthings for children.

The Lenci Company was the brainchild of Enrico and Elena di Scavini of Turin, Italy, and was created shortly after World War I. The Scavini company drew little on other dolls of the time for inspiration. Instead, their influences were the theater, the opera, the Ballets Russes and the Comédie Française. But probably most of all, they reflected the leading fashion illustrators of the day. To be sure, Lenci roses look freshly plucked from the pages of George Barbier, and Lenci geometrics were certainly influenced by the designs of Léon Bakst.

In the Turin workshop, dozens of artists designed and executed these little masterpieces, which probably accounts for the extraordinary range of faces and subjects. Here was a truly creative environment, where no idea was too outrageous to be considered, no possibility too bizarre to be explored.

The medium used was primarily felt (fabrics being the principal product of Turin at the time). Both the dolls and the clothes were made of it (although the dresses were often sprinkled liberally with organdy). There were brief forays into wood and ceramic as base materials, but they never held the place of honor that cloth did.

Lenci dolls first appeared in the U.S. in 1920 (and were concurrently introduced both in Paris and at the Leipzig Fair). Despite their high prices, Lenci dolls sold very well and were a great success until the Great Depression of the 1930s and the ensuing wars (Italy's war with Ethiopia and World War II) curtailed both production and distribution.

Today the company is owned by the Garella family, members of which have worked in the Lenci Company since at least the 1940s. They are actively engaged in making faithful reproductions of the early Lenci dolls. However, it is the beautiful originals—marvelously well preserved, and many never before photographed (or never in color)—which are shown here, and which inspired this book.

The Children

More Lenci dolls were children than any other type made. But within that framework the variety was positively staggering. Expressions varied from piquant to pouty, from surprised to sophisticated, from delighted to depressed. There were no poor waifs here—these children were all well heeled.

The costumes could be elaborate layered pink organdy with felt flower trim, a style that almost became a company trademark, or they could be geometric felt with matching skirts and cloche hats, the fashion trademarks of the time.

Twins and sisters abounded, and when a pair of dolls was intended to be sold together, the eyes of each were painted to glance at those of the other. (Lenci eyes were usually painted glancing left or right, seldom dead center.)

Of the children here, the stylized pouty baby shown at the end of this section is probably the rarest. (For the most part Lenci left realistic baby depiction to the German porcelain dollmakers.)

Most of the dolls pictured still bear their original Lenci tags, and many are in pristine condition. However, most of the tags, which were either metal, cloth or paper, were simply affixed to the costume and have either been purposely removed by the dolls' owners or lost. As a result, Lenci dolls must often be identified by method of construction and look alone.

NOTE: Six additional illustrations from this section appear on the inside front, inside back and back covers.

20″ all-original Lenci child in pink organdy and blue felt costume, 1930s.

10½″ twin girls with eyes glancing at each other; identical costumes.

12″ sisters with eyes glancing at each other; costumes are complementary but not identical.

Rare 16″ baby with face not depicted on any other mold. Number not known.

The Orientals

Chinoiserie, popular throughout the nineteenth century, was once again in vogue in the 1920s. Thus, although never made in abundance, the Orientals were present in the Lenci repertoire from the beginning. (The opium-smoking charmer on the opposite page was used in 1920–21 as part of the official Lenci logo in all advertisements.)

In the Lenci Orientals of the 1920s, the features are stylized and highly exaggerated. The costumes are elaborate, with authentic Oriental designs and trims. Even the hair on these dolls is extraordinarily straight and very black, and feels different in texture from that of other Lencis.

The exceptions appearing in this chapter are the young girl with the German bisque dolly-face look (who seems barely Oriental) and the mascotte (the 9-inch Oriental with surprised round eyes). Both of these were probably made in the 1930s.

Subjects for Oriental dolls were derived from opera (Madame Butterfly) or legend (Dschango) or simply from Oriental art itself (the opium smokers).

At this writing, fewer than ten models of stylized Orientals are known, and very few of those are well preserved, all of which accounts for their extreme rarity.

12″ Oriental opium smoker. Used on Lenci trademark logo in 1920–21. Mint condition.

23″ Lenci geisha, probably late 1920s.

14½″ Oriental girl with German dolly face of the type made in the 1930s.

9″ Oriental mascotte with features that are more mascotte than Oriental, 1930s.

Hu Sun, 23″ opium-smoking woman, mold 251, ca. 1925.

23″ rare and ingenious Lenci Oriental created as a pocketbook.

23″ Dschango, mold 188, with exceptional detail on costume, 1925.

23″ Madame Butterfly, mold 189, with elaborately embroidered costume, 1925.

The Googlies

It was the age of Popeye, Betty Boop and Barney Google with the "goo-goo-googlie eyes." One would have hoped that a company as sophisticated as Lenci would have resisted the mass hysteria, but one would have hoped in vain.

In their mascottes, the 8½-inch dolls with hyperastonished expressions, we find the beginnings of what would come to be known as googlie-eyes. But when collectors speak of a Lenci googlie, what they mean is the large (usually 20-inch) glass-eyed version like the doll pictured opposite.

These dolls, which could be considered scarce, are usually dressed as rich widows in long black silk taffeta dresses, accompanied by their pet dogs. (The source of this costuming is not known; however, the outfits do resemble those worn by some Italian women in mourning.) The other most frequent costume is blue-and-white organdy, cut short like a child's dress. The latter is the version preferred by collectors.

Possibly the rarest of the group pictured here, however, are the widowed sisters, in the same large size as the glass-eyed dolls, but instead with painted eyes. Both ladies have their silver cardboard Lenci tags, as well as their original terrier and dachshund.

20″ glass-eyed Lenci googlie widow with her one-eyed dog, late 1920s.

20″ glass-eyed googlie in rare felt and plaid Scottish costume.

20″ glass-eyed googlie in unusual felt and organdy costume.

Rare pair of 20″ widows with dachshund and terrier. Eyes painted to resemble glass.

20″ glass-eyed googlie in blue organdy, all original. The favorite of most collectors.

The Luscious Ladies

Fashions of the 1920s were chic, they were marvelous and they were certainly divine—and Lenci matched them. Perhaps nowhere is the talent of the Lenci workroom more apparent than in the lady dolls.

Though these long-limbed creatures have bodies resembling what was known in America as "the boudoir doll" (usually a cheap caricature of a 1920s flapper), that is the only resemblance. The Lenci ladies are better compared with the fine French fashion dolls of the 1860s. Not only were they artistically color coordinated, they were often accessorized with purses, gloves and parasols.

The Barbier-inspired Madame de Pompadour gown is a delicious concoction of white organdy and dozens of pink felt rosebuds. Mimi, the "hatbox doll," is a linear gem, beautifully costumed with exquisite detail. The three smaller ladies with simple, mid-calf organdy dresses could have stepped from a lawn party at Scott and Zelda's.

Each face is also distinctive—from the flirtatious Mimi with side-glancing eyes, to Madame de Pompadour smiling inwardly at her own wicked secrets, to the three young ladies who manage to convey their own particular version of sophistication and perhaps a little ennui.

These dolls were usually made in 27- to 29-inch sizes, making the diminutive 15-inch ones exceptionally rare.

Rare and lovely 15″ sloe-eyed lady doll with languid look. Lace mitts are original. Mold number not known, but probably 1920s.

29½″ Mimi, mold 250. Made in 1925, she is in glorious condition.

Choice petite lady, 15″ high. Lenci waistband never removed. Probably late 1920s.

Beautiful 19″ lady doll with lace umbrella. Mold number not known, probably 1930s.

27″ Madame de Pompadour, mold 165. Created in 1927, she is probably the most elaborate Lenci lady ever made.

The Good Sports

The world was mad for sports. The Olympics were the playground of the rich and well traveled. And Lenci dolls, once again, were the imitation of life. While tennis players and golfers appeared most frequently (as they undoubtedly did in real life), those illustrated here are rarer versions than those usually encountered.

The 14-inch girl tennis player opposite, possibly series 450, is less common than the larger (17 inches or more) tennis-playing boys. The series 111 (jumping rope) is also smaller than is usually found. The 8-inch golfer and perfectly matched 6½-inch caddie are seldom seen. Nor is the 7-inch prizefighter, which is much smaller than the listed version of this doll (17½ inches as illustrated in a 1929 advertisement). Even the winter girl dressed for skating is special with her felt coat and muffler, as is the Alpine mountain climber who wears custom boots unique to his sport.

These sports dolls were made for a period of only about five years, from 1925 to 1930. They are seldom discovered in good condition or with their accessories present. In addition to those pictured, Lenci also made polo players, fishermen, baseball heroes, skiers and equestrians.

14″ girl tennis player, possibly series 450, late 1920s.

Very rare 8″ golfer with 6½″ matching caddie. Leather shoes, round cardboard tags, 1920s.

19″ Lenci girl dressed for winter sports in felt coat with muffler.

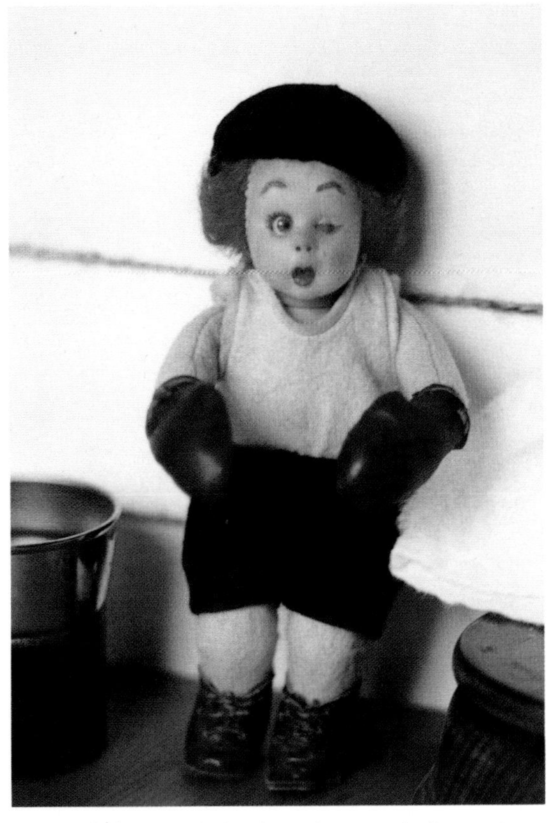

7″ prizefighter with leather shoes and gloves. Late 1920s and very rare.

11″ mountain climber with walking stick, backpack and climber's boots, late 1920s.

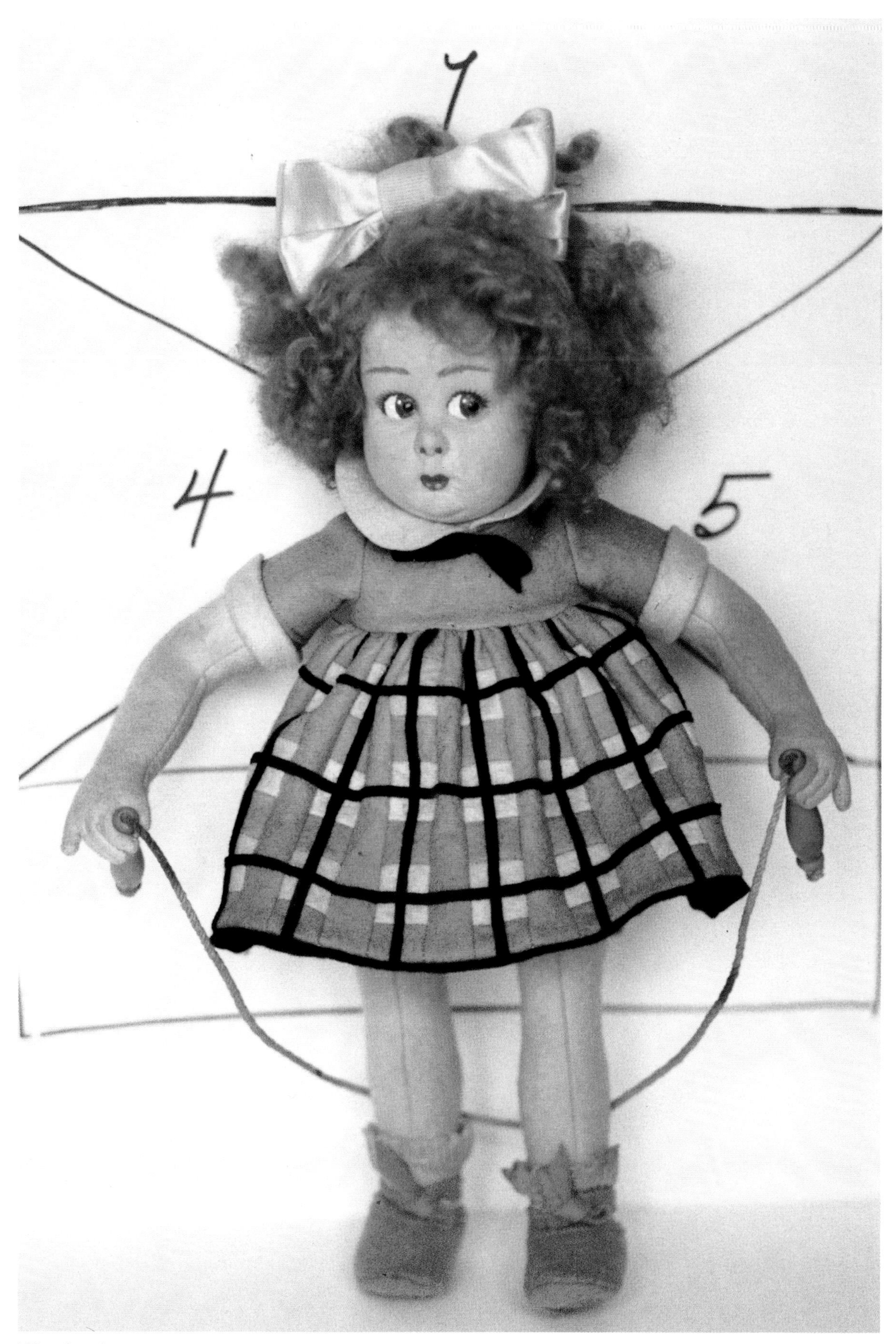

13″ girl with jump rope. Series 111, rope attached, two Lenci tags, 1925.

Fables, Fairy Tales and Fantasies

Collectors, who have their own favorites, may dispute which group in this book represents the Lenci company of the 1920s and 1930s at its best, but there is no doubt about which category gave imagination the freest rein.

The fantasy dolls pictured are just the tip of the iceberg—some have been forgotten until now, and new ones will probably be found tomorrow. Unlike Pan, opposite, the Greek god of shepherds and hunters, which Lenci made in more than one version for many years, most of these were limited editions, most likely made for one year only.

Miss Muffet is a unique Lenci half-doll. Her body is constructed only to the waist, a fact the dress is designed to conceal completely. She came with a matching felt-covered "tuffet" to sit on.

The Goosegirl and Rapunzel both have places in children's fiction but Tom, the small boy on the wooden horse, is a mystery as far as source is concerned. And Bergère is somebody, but one doesn't really know quite who.

Finally, the King and Queen of Marionettes are a rare and recent Lenci find. They are mint, and the Queen wears two Lenci tags. Both the tags and the facial types would place them in the 1930s.

While all the Lenci dolls can certainly be said to display astonishing artistry, it is imaginative pieces like these that occasionally turn up and make Lenci collecting a particularly exciting pastime.

7½" Pan, the Greek god of shepherds and hunters, original pipes. Lenci tags. Made from 1925 on.

14″ Rapunzel with skein of hair. Mint condition. Mold number not known, but 1920s type.

7″ Tom riding a wooden horse and wearing a paper hat. Blue-and-white cloth Lenci tag. Mold number not known.

39″ Bergère, mold 165, made in 1925. Some think this is Bo Peep.

12″ Lenci Goosegirl. Heart-shaped paper tag. Made mid-1930s and later.

14″ Miss Muffet. Rare Lenci half-doll on matching felt-covered "tuffet." Date unknown.

16″ King and Queen of Marionettes. Very choice. Mold number not known, but 1930 types. Queen has two Lenci tags.